BIRD
watching

ICELAND NATURE GUIDES

BIRD
watching

text:
HELGI GUÐMUNDSSON
JÓN BALDUR HLÍÐBERG

illustrations:
JÓN BALDUR HLÍÐBERG

RITSMIÐJAN

TO THE READER

This publication is not a bird guide in the conventional sense, but is intended to help birdwatchers find suitable places for birdwatching. The book includes brief and accessible details of some of the areas of Iceland that are best known for their rich bird life. The authors have many years of experience guiding people with an interest in nature around Iceland, and they are familiar with the places which are most interesting to birdwatchers.

The first part of the book gives an account of the Icelandic landscape and seasonal weather conditions. This is followed by a description of twelve areas, of different size, where many suitable birdwatching locations are detailed. Then each individual species is briefly discussed. At the back of the book is a checklist of over 120 bird species.

This book was first conceived as a supplementary guide for birdwatchers in Iceland. Because such birdwatching travellers are likely to be well-informed about the birds themselves but to need some further information about general and regional conditions, we felta handbook of this kind was both necessary and desirable. We also hope that, with growing awareness of environmental issues, this book will be of interest to all visitors who have come to realise the importance of their environment and their relationship with nature.

Helgi Guðmundsson
Jón B. Hlíðberg

Birdwatching © Text: Helgi Guðmundsson and Jón Baldur Hlíðberg
Illustration: Jón Baldur Hlíðberg Publisher: Ritsmiðjan, Reykjavík 1997 • Translation: Anna Yates
Cover design: Soffía frænka • Films: Offsetþjónustan • Printed and bound in Portugal
Mapmaking by kind permission of the National Landsurvey of Iceland
Special thanks to Icelandair for their support

ISBN 9979-9296-1-8

CONTENTS

BIRD LIFE AND ICELANDIC CONDITIONS

Iceland is an island in the north Atlantic and counted the westernmost part of Europe. It is 780 km to the nearest point in the British Isles, and 970 km to Norway. West of Iceland, the closest point on the east coast of Greenland is 290 km away.

Iceland's area is a little more than 100,000 km²

Iceland's area is a little more than 100,000 km². Much of the island consists of uninhabitable mountain territory, and in many places this reaches out to the coast. A little more than 10% of the country is covered by glaciers, and a similar expanse by lava fields of the Holocene epoch. The coast of Iceland is deeply indented, with the exception of the south coast. Principal lowland areas are in the south, in Borgarfjörður in the west, and in the Fljótsdalur region in the east. Other lowland areas generally consist of a coastal strip, and valleys at the heads of fjords. There are many lakes, most of them small. Iceland also has innumerable rivers, of which the largest are glacial rivers. Iceland has a cool temperate maritime climate. Due to the influence of the Gulf Stream, the climate is fairly mild, with no great difference between average temperatures in summer and winter; the Icelandic summer is fairly cool.

Flora

The country is rather barren, and almost treeless. In lowland areas there are many marshes and moors, with skrubs here and there. Vegetation, however, has been subjected to considerable disturbance in recent decades due to the draining of marshes for agriculture and to the centuries-old process of desertification (caused both by man and by harsh natural conditions). The island's nature and location may thus actually be a hindrance to a diverse bird life. In this context, a factor is the lack of forests, and also of the insect life on which many birds live.

About 70 bird species breed regularly in Iceland, many of which only spend three to five months in the country each year; others are residents. In total 30 species have been added to Iceland's bird population during this century, though only eight of these have established themselves. Although only a small number of species breed in Iceland, the population of some species is so large that Iceland may be counted as rich in bird life. The vast majority of the species breed also in neighbouring European countries, or around the Arctic region. Three species, the great northern diver or the common loon, the Barrow's goldeneye and the harlequin duck, have come to Iceland from North America, and Iceland is their only breeding location in Europe.

An island rich in bird life

By far the majority of Iceland's birds are seabirds and various species of wetland birds, which account for about two-thirds of all Iceland's breeding species. Seabird populations are the largest, as conditions are particularly favourable to them with plentiful food in the ocean, and excellent nesting grounds on sea cliffs and innumerable islands. The same applies to wetland birds, although their habitats undergone substantial erosion in recent decades. Large-scale draining of marshes is one of the most serious threats to Iceland's bird life. On the continents on either side of the Atlantic, passerines are the commonest birds, but in Iceland the reverse is true; only about 10 species of passerines breed regularly in Iceland.

Some species, known as passage migrants, stop over in Iceland in spring and autumn on their migration between the breeding grounds, north of Iceland, and their winter home farther south. There are also a number of vagrant species, most of which are rarely spotted, although some vagrants are annual visitors, and may even visit Iceland in groups. A total of over 330 bird species have been observed at least once in Iceland, most of them vagrants.

Over 330 bird species have been observed

BIRDWATCHING BY SEASONS

Winter In the winter, birds tend to keep close to the coast, and an astonishing range of birds may be observed by the sea, where they can survive a harsh winter. At this time of year, gulls and eiders are predominant, but various duck species may also be seen. Waders and passerines are also seen on the shore, while offshore one may see cormorants, skuas and auks, and the occasional diver (loon). Fewer species can be observed inland, but ducks may be seen on lakes and streams that are not frozen. One may often see a ptarmigan, and the gyr falcon is often nearby. But the birds one is most likely to come across inland at this season are the snow bunting and the raven.

Spring With the coming of spring, the bird population rises. The first migratory birds arrive in February; migration peaks in April and early May. By the end of May, all the migratory birds have arrived in Iceland. In spring, the shore teems with life, as most migrants pause there on arrival in Iceland. In addition, several migratory species stop over in Iceland on their way to their breeding grounds north of the Arctic circle, such as the knot, sanderling and turnstone. In the west, flocks of brent geese gather on mudflats, and the barnacle goose may be seen on meadows in the north. This period is followed by the breeding season, a sensitive time in the bird's life. All movement in breeding grounds disturbs the birds, and may have a serious impact upon them. It is normally possible to deduce from the bird's behaviour whether they are nesting; in which case, they should be approached with great care.

Surprisingly, perhaps, mid-summer is not the best **Summer**
season for birdwatching, as many birds leave their
breeding grounds at the end of the breeding season.
At about this time, drakes gather into groups to moult.
They shed their breeding finery, so they are less
colourful in late summer. By the beginning of August
most of the birds have flown out to sea or to other
countries. Auks, for instance, have mostly left the
birdcliffs by the end of the first week in August. Bird
behaviour is also less noticeable in late summer, as
most tend to keep a low profile.

In early autumn, various species gather together in **Autumn**
preparation for their migration. Fields are full of
geese, swans and golden plovers, while on the shore
are thousands of purple sandpipers and dunlins, as
well as other migratory species (both Icelandic breeding species and passage migrants). The autumn is the
favourite season of many birdwatchers, but it is also
more demanding than other seasons. An enormous
number of different species can be seen, in diverse
colourings. This is also the prime time for observing
various rare species. Small groups of vagrants can
sometimes be seen in the autumn, but they are usual- Barrow's goldeneye
ly quite elusive.

WHERE TO WATCH BIRDS

This chapter gives brief descriptions of the areas in Iceland most rewarding for the birdwatcher, but they are by no means exhaustive. There are many locations all over the country where birds are easy to find, and it would be impossible to include them all in a publication such as this.

In general, we focus on the period from April to September – from the arrival of migratory species in spring to their departure in autumn. Recommendations regarding other seasons are made where applicable.

The birdwatching areas mentioned are almost all accessible by road. Beginning with the southwest region of the country, this guide follows the coast clockwise around the island. Details of road access are given in each section; roads are specified by number where applicable, and in some cases the roads may be open for a limited period of the year, etc. This is followed by a short description of the environment, e.g. vegetation and water sources, and then a general account of the bird life of the area, and a list of the species which are typical for the area, or which have unusual status.

Various areas which are off the beaten track are not listed, although they include some of Iceland's major bird colonies. The islands of Drangey and Grímsey off the north coast, however, are worth mentioning. Grímsey was, at least at least until recently, the last breeding location of the little auk on Iceland's shores. Also worthy of mention are Hornbjarg and Hælavíkurbjarg in the West Fjords and Langanes in the northeast, where vast numbers of birds cluster on huge birdcliffs. The pink-footed goose breeds in larger numbers in the Icelandic highlands than anywhere else. They can be found mainly in Þjórsárver south of the Hofsjökull glacier, but also in the highlands of the north and east. In recent years, regular transportation has been available to most of the places named here, at least in summer.

Finally, readers of this guide are reminded to follow all conservation laws. Some locations are designated as conservation areas due to their bird life, and may be closed during the breeding season, either in whole or in part.

Breeding areas must be approached with care. Careless behaviour may disturb the birds and disrupt their breeding. Also, in some cases bird colonies are a resource utilised by man, e.g. egg-gathering on bird cliffs, and eider colonies for their down. In such cases, the permission of the land-owner should be sought before approaching the birds.

The nests of a few rare species are specifically protected, and it is prohibited to approach their nests to take pictures, make recordings, study the birds, or for other purposes that may be expected to disturb them. These species are the gyr falcon, white-tailed eagle, snowy owl, little auk, water rail and grey phalarope.

Red-throated diver

1.
REYKJANES PENINSULA
(outer region)

Reykjanes is an area of volcanic rock and lava, with many clefts and gorges; it lies on the margin of the Eurasian and north American plates, and is directly connected to the mid-Atlantic ridge. Along the shore, low cliffs alternate with sandy beaches, where ocean waves sweep unhindered onto the coast.

This area is affected by the many low-pressure areas that move over Iceland from the southwest; hence the climate is changeable and precipitation quite high.

Vegetation is rather sparse and monotonous. The wild flora consist largely of mosses, heathers and hardy grasses.

Adjacent to the Reykjanes lighthouse, there is a large and easily accessible colony of arctic terns. Off the shore is Eldey island, where Iceland's largest gannet colony is located. Just off the coast is a rock pillar, Karlinn (the Old Man), where gannets are also found, although they do not breed there.

Farther along the coast is a bird cliff, Hafnaberg, where all the auk species that breed in Iceland may be found, with the exception of the little auk. There are also many kittiwakes, as well as cormorants and other species. From road no. 425 a signposted footpath leads down to the clifftop.

How to get there:
The area is easily accessible at all times of year, and within reach of the capital city. It is quite possible to visit all the principal birdwatching locations in one day, even taking in the south of area no 2. (Reykjavík area), i.e. Álftanes and Ástjörn.

At the harbour in Hafnir, both harlequin ducks and great northern divers may be seen in winter, and many other bird species at all seasons of the year.

The shore at Sandgerði has a thriving bird population, while ducks and waders may be spotted on ponds and lagoons. Those who are interested in learning more about the nature and history of the area should visit the Fræðasetur nature centre in Sandgerði.

Garðskagi, the peninsula at the outermost point of the Reykjanes peninsula, is an important staging post for many migratory birds heading farther north such as the knot, turnstone and sanderling. This location is well known to birdwatchers, both in Iceland and abroad. At migration seasons, the shore at the lighthouse teems with even more birds than usual, often including various vagrant species.

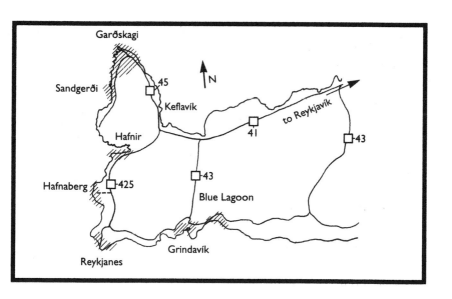

2.
REYKJAVÍK AND VICINITY

Many bird habitats have disappeared due to construction and development; nonetheless, almost untouched shores and mudflats may still be found close to the city. In the Reykjavík area, the number of bird species has risen somewhat in recent decades, as arboriculture has increased. Convenient places within the City of Reykjavík include e.g. the forestry plantation in Fossvogur, and woods adjacent to the Botanical Gardens in Laugardalur, and in Elliðaárdalur.

The downtown Lake is rich in bird life; on the marshes to the south of the Lake, greylag geese, ducks and other wetland birds breed, while arctic terns, black-headed gulls, whooper swans and ducks nest on the islet in the middle of the Lake. Other birdwatching locations are the estuary of the Elliðaá river, Grafarvogur, and the mudflats of Arnarvogur and Kópavogur.

It is well worth making a trip out to the offshore island of Viðey, a peaceful place where many bird species breed. In summer, for instance, puffins may often be seen on the sea off the north end of the island. A ferry plies several times daily between Viðey and the mainland; the trip across to the island takes only about five minutes. Excursions are also offered by boat from Reykjavík in the summer to Lundey (Puffin island).

Finally, beyond the city limits is the outer area of the Seltjarnarnes peninsula, and the shore by the island of Grótta. At low tide, it is possible to walk out to the island. At Grótta is an arctic tern colony, which is protected during the breeding season.

All year round, many seabird species stay on the shore around Reykjavík: the Iceland gull, for instance, is common in winter. These birds spend the summer in Greenland, where they breed.

How to get there:
Most locations named are within walking distance of bus routes.

The Álftanes peninsula, south of Reykjavík, is a popular birdwatching spot. Many species breed at Álftanes, such as the arctic tern, eider duck, and other ducks and waders. In addition, many passage migrants pass through in spring and autumn, especially the knot and brent goose.

Farther south along the coast, e.g. at the harbour in the town of Hafnarfjörður, various species of ducks, waders and seabirds are seen. Here a larger variety of species may be seen in winter than in summer.

Ástjörn, a lake above the town of Hafnarfjörður, is the only breeding place in southwest Iceland of the horned or Slavonian grebe. The species has declined somewhat in recent decades, and the horned grebe now breeds in few places other than the Mývatn region of the northeast.

Inland are the lakes of Urriðakotsvatn, Vífilsstaðavatn and Elliðavatn. The great northern diver normally breeds at Elliðavatn every year.

The southern limit of the area is at Straumsvík. In the inlet by the aluminium plant there are often many ducks, swans and various species of seabirds.

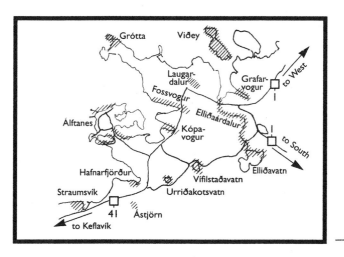

3.
MÝRAR AND SNÆFELLSNES PENINSULA

The route through Mýrar and the Snæfellsnes peninsula passes through country which is quite well covered by vegetation. This is mostly meadow and moorland vegetation, along with marshland. Low-growing shrubs are seen in some places, though very sparsely. There are many rivers, streams and small ponds, many of them close to the road.

Most noticeable are moorland birds and waterbirds. The main road runs partly along the coast, so it is possible to observe birdlife both on the shore and on dry land.

In Mýrar, many red-throated divers may be seen on lakes and ponds, and one is likely to come across an occasional horned grebe. The area also boasts of water- and sea-birds, in addition to waders that gather in their thousands on the mudflats at the shore to feed. The Mýrar-Snæfellsnes region is also part of the distribution area of the white-tailed eagle.

The vast majority of Iceland's mudflats and beaches are on the west coast, and hence more varied birdlife may be expected here than in most other areas. This applies especially to the migration season, when many species migrate between breeding grounds north of the Arctic Circle and their winter homes in mainland Europe and farther south. Their migration

How to get there:
In order to have enough time to see the area properly, it is advisable to plan for at least two days. The area is easily accessible from Reykjavík. From the main road through the Mýrar district (no. 54), several roads lead down to the coast, e.g. roads no. 533 and 540.

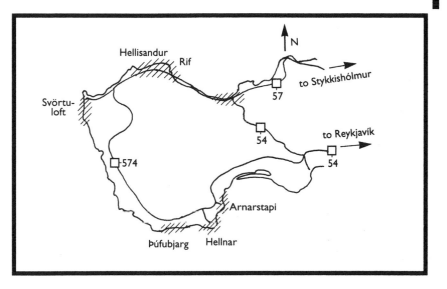

route passes over the west coast of Iceland, and various coastal areas, beaches and mudflats on the west coast are important sources of nutrition for these species.

Along the south coast of the Snæfellsnes peninsula there are many small lakes and ponds close to the road, where birds are generally to be found, e.g. whooper swans, ducks and divers, as well as many other birds, especially arctic terns, black-headed gulls and various species of waders.

The coast between Arnarstapi and Hellnar is famous for its bizarre rock formations and its huge bird population. Most noticeable are the kittiwake and arctic tern, while the great black-backed gull and other gulls also breed there. The occasional auk may be seen offshore, as well as harlequin ducks in the powerful waves beneath the bird cliffs, and a few red-necked phalaropes on small ponds.

A short distance beyond Hellnar is Þúfubjarg, part of an old volcanic crater, a birdcliff where kittiwakes, guillemots and fulmars breed.

Area 3.
Tip of Snæfellsnes peninsula

Farther north is Svörtuloft, a fairly high sea cliff, where various species of seabirds breed, such as auks, fulmars and kittiwakes. The road to Svörtuloft is difficult in places, but the landscape is spectacular.

The road between Hellissandur and Rif passes through one of Iceland's greatest arctic tern colonies. Shallow ponds near the crossroads at Rif are worth looking at. Many coastal birds are found here, and also on the coastal ridge along the road to Ólafsvík, e.g. eider duck, purple sandpiper, dunlin, arctic tern and red-necked Phalarope.

On the north coast of the Snæfellsnes peninsula, the glaucous gull is very noticeable; this is part of the species' principal breeding area, and in some places bright green vegetation may be seen at glaucous gull colonies high up on mountain slopes.

On islands and skerries, which number thousands in the Breiðafjörður bay north of Snæfellsnes, a vast number of seabirds breed, including puffins and other auks. Breiðafjörður is also the principal breeding ground of the cormorant and shag. A few pairs of white-tailed eagles also breed in the area. In olden times, many of the islands were inhabited, and eider down and sea-bird hunting were important resources. Eider colonies are still exploited on some of the islands. Regular ferry services operate all year round between Stykkishólmur on the Snæfellsnes peninsula and Brjánslækur, calling at Flatey island. In summer, daily sightseeing cruises of the islands operate from Stykkishólmur.

On Álftafjörður (Swan Fjord), east of Stykkishólmur, about a thousand whooper swans may be seen in summer, along with many other bird species.

4.
THE LÁTRABJARG BIRDCLIFF AND SURROUNDINGS

The road from Patreksfjörður to Örlygshöfn passes along steep screes, which lead to a valley with a sea lagoon. There is little lowland here, as elsewhere in the West Fjords, and the land is rather barren. There is, however, some grassland and moorland in the bays, and light-coloured shell-sand beaches in some places along the shore. There is a large eider colony at Örlygshöfn.

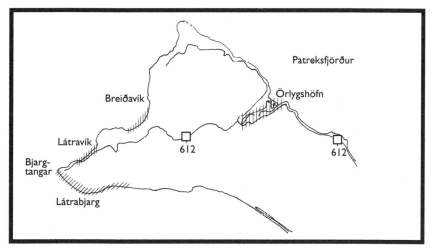

How to get there:
Roads in the West Fjords region pass over heathland and through mountain passes, and are hence often closed by snow in winter. The road (no. 612) from the head of Patreksfjörður to Bjargtangar, Iceland's westernmost point, is rough in places, and must be travelled with care, but is passable to all vehicles in summer. The road reaches to the Bjargtangaviti lighthouse, and from here one can walk along the clifftop of Látrabjarg. Regular bus services operate between Látrabjarg and the main towns of the West Fjords during the summer. This is an ideal trip from Ísafjörður, although rather long for a one-day excursion.

From Örlygshöfn, the route continues over the heathland above Breiðavík to Látravík and Bjargtangar. Breiðavík has many marsh birds, such as the redthroated diver, whooper swan and red-necked Phalarope, while Látravík has many ringed plovers. In the upland, the snow bunting is the most noticeable species.

The road ends at Bjargtangar, the westernmost point of Europe. On leaving the car, the first thing one seesare puffins, standing on the cliff edge. Bear in mind that the turf of the cliffs is riddled with puffin burrows, so one should tread carefully.

Látrabjarg is Iceland's greatest bird cliff, and also the largest in the north Atlantic. The cliff is about 14 km long and about 450 metres at its highest point.

It has been estimated that up to a million birds of various species nest on Látrabjarg; the density of the nesting colonies varies. All the auk species known in Iceland nest here, with the exception of the Little Auk. At the bottom of Látrabjarg is the largest continuous razorbill colony in the world. In addition to auks there are also many fulmars and kittiwakes.

Razorbill

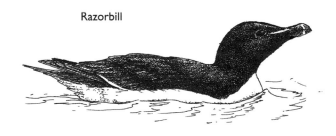

5.
ÍSAFJARÐARDJÚP

The landscape of the northern West Fjords is similar to the southern part of the region. There is little lowland, and in many places there are perpendicular cliffs at the sea's edge. The inner part of Ísafjarðardjúp, however, has more vegetation than most other parts of the region. There are birch copses, for instance, on mountainsides and valleys, and there are many verdant islands such as Æðey (Eider island), Vigur and others. The environment is thus somewhat milder and gentler in the inner reaches of Ísafjarðardjúp.

A vast number of eiders, puffins and other seabirds breed on the islands. Æðey is now only inhabited in summer, but the eider colony is utilised there, as on Vigur, which is inhabited all year round.

It is worth stopping from time to time along the shore to look around for a long-tailed duck or goosander. Harlequin ducks may also be seen in many places by rivers and brooks. Wrens and ptarmigans are among the species that may be seen in birch copses. And a few pairs of white-tailed eagles breed in Ísafjarðardjúp.

In Vatnsfjörður and Reykjanes are marsh areas where birdlife is varied.

How to get there:
The places on land that are mentioned here all have good road connections. In addition, there are regular ferry services all year, as well as sightseeing cruises from Ísafjörður around Ísafjarðardjúp and as far as Hornstrandir during the summer. At Hornstrandir are some of Iceland's greatest colonies of cliff birds. An ideal excursion from Ísafjörður.

6.
LAKE MÝVATN AND THE LAXÁ RIVER

The area is at the western edge of a volcanic zone that passes across the country. The volcanic area of the north is part of a very active zone on the margin of the Eurasian and north American plates. Eruptions are frequent, and this has made its mark on the landscape. Geological formations are recent, and lava and volcanoes are an important part of the landscape.

Lake Mývatn (Midge Lake) was created in its present form by a lava flow about two thousand years ago. The shores of the lake are highly indented, and there are dozens of islands, large and small. The Laxá river, that flows out of Lake Mývatn, follows the course of the lava flow to the sea.

Lake Mývatn is one of Iceland largest lakes. It lies at about 280 metres above sea level, and is rather shallow. It is thus highly sensitive to changes of temperature and climate. The catchment area of the lake consists largely of lava and sand, so water courses are largely underground. The flow of water into Lake Mývatn is largely from many freshwater springs on its eastern shore. The lake is rich in nutrients, and sustains a huge population of midges, from which it derives its name. Along with the midges, various minute aquatic organisms play a vital role in the food chain of the lake, and Lake Mývatn abounds in trout.

Lake Mývatn is about 50 km from the sea, and oceanic influences are thus less than at the coast. The climate of the area is more continental, and this has its influ-

How to get there:
Communications by road and air are good all year round. An ideal day excursion e.g. from Akureyri or Húsavík, or by air from Reykjavík.

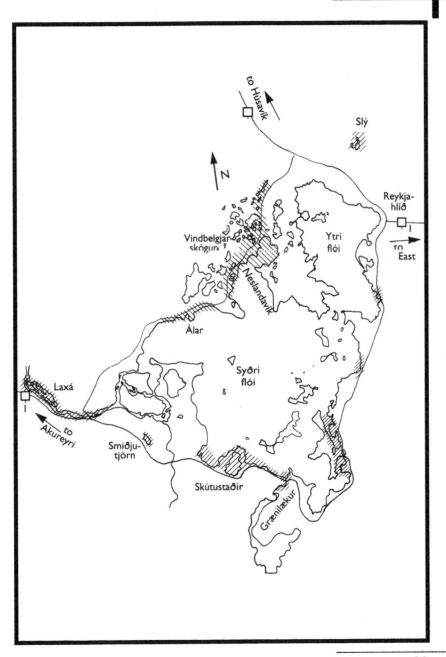

ence upon vegetation, which is quite varied. The shores of the lake are grassy, and birch copses are widespread.

Lake Mývatn is world famous for its bird life. At the lake itself and on the Laxá river, all Iceland's duck species breed, and there are few places in the world with such a varied duck population. Many other bird species also breed here, including water birds, moor birds etc. There are arctic terns, black-headed gulls, red-necked phalaropes and various waders. Among other species which are less numerous and noticeable are e.g. the great northern and red-throated divers, and horned or Slavonian grebe. The gyr falcon, merlin and ptarmigan may also be seen.

Two American species, the Barrow's goldeneye and harlequin duck, are very common breeders at Lake Mývatn and the Laxá river; Iceland is their only breeding place in Europe.

Convenient birdwatching locations include Höfði and Kálfastrandavogar, also the shore and headland at Skútustaðir, and the banks of the Laxá river. On the northern shore of Lake Mývatn are many inlets and ponds with a large bird population, to mention but a few places. Note that some of the breeding areas are, at least in part, closed to pedestrian traffic off roads and paths during the nesting season, i.e. for about six weeks each summer.

Great northern diver

7.
THE EAST
(Fljótsdalshérað and the East Fjords
from Reyðarfjörður to Höfn)

Much of Fljótsdalshérað is at some distance from the sea, and is sheltered by mountains and highlands on both sides. The climate is thus relatively stable, and larger birch woods are found here than elsewhere in the country.

Fljótsdalshérað reaches the sea at Héraðsflói, where there are extensive sandy shores, and marshy areas with brooks, lakes and sedge meadows which have been drained only to a small degree. The great skua is common near the sea, while farther inland are large numbers of arctic skuas, red-throated divers and various moorland birds, especially whimbrels. Whimbrels breed more densely here than anywhere else in Iceland. Up the large rivers, Jökulsá á Dal and Héraðsvötn, there are considerable populations of greylag geese and pink-footed geese.

The birch woods of Fljótsdalshérað have similar bird species to other wooded areas of Iceland. Various vagrants are also frequently seen here, such as the crossbill.

The route to the coast passes over the East Fjords mountain range, which is about 800 to 1200 metres high. Many narrow fjords cut inland between high, steep mountains, and the road weaves along the

How to get there:
Good communications all year round. An excursion from Egilsstaðir to the locations mentioned in Fljótsdalshérað is ideal as a day trip. The same applies to Höfn, Hornafjörður and the south of the area, i.e. from Hvalnesskriður to Hornafjörður.

Arctic skua

headlands and fjords. There is little lowland in the East Fjords, but more towards the south.

Places of interest for the birdwatcher include the islands of Skrúður and Papey which lie just offshore. Gannets and puffins breed on Skrúður, as well as many other seabird species, while Papey is largely a puffin and eider colony. Sightseeing tours operate to Papey in summer from the fishing village of Djúpivogur, but Skrúður is less accessible, as it is far more difficult to land on the island.

The road runs between Álftafjörður (Swan Fjord) and Lónsfjörður. These fjords are shallow, with abundant vegetation on the sea floor, as well as salt marshes, ponds and marshes. These are important staging posts for migratory birds, while in summer the whooper swan is the predominant species and may be seen in its thousands on sea lagoons.

On the sea below the road along Hvalnesskriður one may generally see masses of eider ducks. The common scoter also spends much of the year in this area.

Hornafjörður, Skarðsfjörður and Stokknes are at the southern limit of this area. Around Höfn in Hornafjörður is abundant bird life, e.g. in Skarðsfjörður, a shallow saltwater lagoon with islands, skerries and mudflats which teem with life. Breeding birds here include the puffin and eider. At Stokknes there are large arctic tern and eider colonies. Various other species also breed here, such as the ringed plover and red-necked phalarope.

8.
HÖFN TO SKAFTAFELL

The area consists of alternating sandy regions and agricultural land, with an admixture of marshes and bogs. Lakes, ponds and saltwater lagoons are found along the route, which passes over many rivers, many of them glacial rivers carrying a large volume of water.

In the eastern part of the area, marsh birds are predominant, e.g. whooper swans, ducks and waders, as well as arctic terns and black-headed gulls. In the spring, many migratory birds are first spotted in this region, and various vagrants may be seen here during the migration season, The migration route of the barnacle goose passes through the southeast, and some barnacle geese have bred in the region in recent years.

Breiðamerkursandur is the principal breeding ground of the great skua in Iceland, and a vast number of Arctic Skuas also breed in the area, in addition to other bird species. Along the road across the sands, red-throated divers may be seen on ponds.

Finally, many seabirds breed on Ingólfshöfði, a rocky headland where gannets may be seen. Leach's petrels have also been known to breed there in recent years. It is easy to reach Ingólfshöfði with the assistance of local residents, who operate sightseeing tours in summer. It is inadvisable to attempt to reach the headland without assistance.

The Skaftafell National Park is a natural beauty spot between glacier and barren sands. The birch woods echo with the song of Redwings and Wrens, and on the heathland beyond one may see ptarmigans and snow buntings.

How to get there:
Good communications all year round. An ideal day excursion from Höfn, Hornafjörður and Skaftafell.

9.
VÍK AND DYRHÓLAEY

The area is open to the ocean; sands and marshes alternate with sea cliffs. This is the southernmost region of Iceland, and the Dyrhólaey headland is its southernmost point. Low-pressure areas regularly move over the country from the south, bringing windy and rainy weather.

By the main road just east of the village of Vík is one of Iceland's largest arctic tern colonies, while masses of fulmars nest on the cliffs above the road. The area in general has plentiful fulmar breeding grounds. On Mt. Reynisfjall near Vík is a puffin colony, and some guillemots breed on Reynisdrangar, rock pillars just offshore from Reynisfjall.

There are sizable puffin and arctic colonies on the rock headland of Dyrhólaey, as well as guillemots and other seabird species.

Great skuas and arctic skuas nest on the sands along the sea shore, and marsh birds in the marshy areas farther inland.

Young tern

How to get there:
Good communications all year round. An ideal day excursion from the Reykjavík area. Note that the Dyrhólaey headland itself is closed to all visitors during the breeding season, i.e. about six weeks of each summer.

10.
WESTMAN ISLANDS

The Westman Islands, off the south coast of Iceland, are rocky, steep-sided islands which were mostly formed by undersea volcanic eruptions. They number nearly twenty, in addition to which there are about thirty rock pillars and skerries in the sea around the islands. The youngest island of the archipelago is Surtsey, which was formed in the 1960s. About ten years later, volcanic activity broke out on Heimaey, the largest of the islands. This indicates that this is an active volcanic zone. The islands are largely of pyroclastite, while they are generally grassy on top. Only one island, Heimaey, is inhabited; this is one of Iceland's most important fishing ports.

Black guillemot

How to get there:

Regular transport is available daily between the mainland and the Westman Islands, by air from Reykjavík, and by ferry from Þorlákshöfn west of the city. There are also air services between the Westman Islands and the Bakki airport in the southern mainland. On reaching the islands, various sightseeing options are available, both on sea and on land. If one flies from Reykjavík on an early flight, there is plenty of time to see the islands and return to Reykjavík in the evening. It is also possible to fly one way and travel back by sea. It is worth visiting the Westman Islands Natural Science Museum, which has a good collection of stuffed birds, and also a selection of live fish and other marine creatures.

Conditions in the sea off the Westman Islands are remarkably favourable, offering plentiful food for birds. Hence a vast number of seabirds breed here, including all the auk species that breed in Iceland, with the exception of the little auk. The Westman Islands are the most populous puffin breeding ground in the world, with millions of puffins in the summer. Gannets breed on some islands and rock pillars.

The Westman Islands are the only breeding place of the manx shearwater in Iceland, and the same applied until recently to the Leach's petrel and storm petrel. Iceland is the northernmost breeding place of these three species in the world.

Kittiwake

II.
THE SOUTH COAST BETWEEN THE ÞJÓRSÁ AND ÖLFUSÁ RIVERS

Along the low-lying, flat coast are many brooks and ponds; marshes and bogs alternate with cultivated land, while there are sandy shores adjacent to the river estuaries that form the limits of the area. Beneath the soil of the lowlands lies an extensive lava field, Þjórsárhraun. The edge of the lava field stretches some hundreds of metres into the sea, protecting the land from erosion. The ocean waves break on the edge of the lava, while within the barrier the sea is calmer in channels between the skerries.

The area is rich in bird life, mostly marsh birds and seabirds. This is an interesting birdwatching region at all seasons, not least during spring, when flocks of migrating birds may be seen flying in from the sea to land on the shore. There may also be many birds in the area in winter, e.g. the great northern and red-throated divers, various gulls and ducks, and even auks close inshore. At any time of year one may come across vagrants and passage migrants.

Although the coastal section from the Þjórsá river to the Ölfusá river is regarded as a single area, some places deserve more attention than others, e.g. the section from Knarrarósviti to Stokkseyri, the shore at Stokkseyri and Eyrarbakki, and the estuary of the Ölfusá river.

Until recently, one of the few breeding grounds of the

How to get there:
Good communications all year round, within reach of the Reykjavík area. It is quite feasible to see all the principal locations in one day, even including area no. 12 (Þingvallavatn and Sog) in the same excursion.

grey phalarope in Iceland was at the mouth of the Hraunsá river, midway between Stokkseyri and Eyrarbakki.

Areas 11 and 12

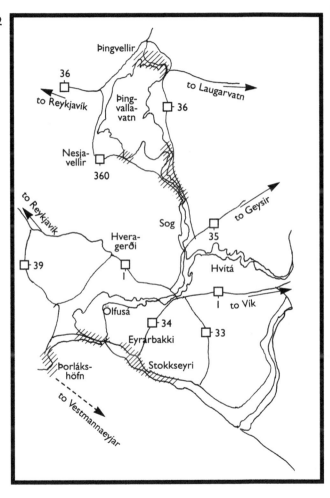

12.
LAKE ÞINGVALLAVATN AND THE SOG RIVER

Þingvallavatn (Þingvellir Lake), one of Iceland's biggest and deepest lakes, is located in a large, elongated rift valley that stretches from southwest to northeast from Mt. Hengill to the Langjökull glacier. The lake is largely formed by spring water, which brings with it many substances and compounds from the bedrock that are important to the ecosystem of the lake. The ecosystem of the lake is particularly rich; it is in fact unique for this latitude. From the southern end of Þingvallavatn flows Sog, Iceland's largest spring-fed river. In places Sog is fairly wide, forming the "lakes" Úlfljótsvatn and Álftavatn, where the river bed is widest. There is trout in the Sog river, and also salmon in the lower reaches, above the confluence with the Hvítá river.

Although the Þingvallavatn lake freezes over in the latter part of winter, i.e. from the end of January to late April, a section at the northern end of the lake normally remains unfrozen, where spring water flows into the lake all year round at a constant temperature.

The same applies to Sog; some sections of the river never freeze, even in the harshest winter. These places thus tend to attract birds at that time of the year.

Hydro-electric power plants have had some effect upon the water level of the Þingvallavatn lake and the course of the Sog river.

How to get there:
The area is easy of access at all times of year, and within reach of the Reykjavík area. It is quite feasible to visit all the main locations in a single day, even taking in area no. 11 (from the estuary of the Þjórsá river to that of the Ölfusá river) on the same trip.

The vegetation of the Þingvallavatn area is quite varied, with heather and birch copses, as well as grass and marshes in places. Along the Sog, the river banks are grassy right down to the surface of the water; the flow of the river remains fairly constant all year round.

The bird life of the area is varied. Water birds include great northern and red-throated divers, greylag goose, Barrow's goldeneye, harlequin duck, goosander and other duck species. There are also many moorland birds, such as the redwing, wren and ptarmigan.

Particularly good locations include the national park of Þingvellir, and the northern shores of the lake, as well as Hestvík and Hagavík at its southern end.

The most important locations below Þingvallavatn are Úlfljótsvatn and the reservoir of the Ljósafoss and Írafoss hydro-electric plants. Harlequin ducks are found on the Sog river, especially in spring, and from the bridge where the main road crosses the river, down to the confluence of the Sog and Hvítá rivers one may see various duck species at all times of year. In winter one may often see goldeneyes on the Sog. These are regular annual winter visitors, but are not known to have bred in Iceland.

Black-tailed godwit

ICELANDIC BIRD SPECIES

This section gives information on all the bird species that breed regularly in Iceland. In addition, passage migrants, winter visitors and common vagrants that the birdwatcher may come across are mentioned. To include all the species that have been seen at some time in Iceland would take too much space, and this volume is not intended to be an exhaustive guide. With regard to identifying species, we suggest the use of a bird guide; in the following list, the conventional taxonomic order used in bird guides is followed.

DIVERS
(Gaviidae)

Two Icelandic species belong to the order of divers, the great northern diver, known in north America as the common loon (Gavia immer) and the red-throated diver, whose American name is the red-throated loon (Gavia stellata). These birds breed in all parts of the country, but their nesting preferences are somewhat different.

Great northern diver

The **great northern diver** nests on the banks of trout rivers, where food is plentiful. While the great northern diver cannot be called a common bird, it is rather noticeable, especially inland. On still summer evenings, the great northern diver's wails can be heard over long distances.

The **red-throated diver** normally nests by shallow ponds, sometimes in groups; they gather food from both lakes and the sea.

An occasional individual of both species may spend the winter on the coast of Iceland, and they can sometimes be seen just offshore.

GREBES
(Podicipedidae)

The horned or **Slavonian grebe** (Podiceps auritus) is the only representative of the grebes in Iceland. Horned grebes nest by lakes and ponds with plentiful organic life; this is the only Icelandic bird to make a floating nest. The horned grebe population has fallen sharply in recent decades, and it is not common in any part of the country except at Lake Mývatn and its surroundings.

Slavonian grebe

FULMARS AND SHEARWATERS
(Procellariidae)

The fulmar (Fulmarus glacialis) is one of Iceland's commonest breeding birds, whose population has risen enormously in recent decades. Fulmar colonies can now be found on almost all mountains and cliffs by the shore, and there are also examples of fulmar colonies as far as 50 km inland.

The manx shearwater (Puffinus puffinus), a member of the Procellariidae, nests only in the Westman Islands. They may often be seen in large flocks on the sea, e.g. off Ystiklettur. This species is otherwise rarely seen from dry land.

Manx shearwaters

Two other Procellariidae species are seen from time to time in Iceland, **the great shearwater** (Puffinus gravis), now very rare, and **the sooty shearwater** (Puffinus griseus), a regular annual vagrant. These species breed in the southern hemisphere, and fly to the north in June and July.

PETRELS
(Hydrobatidae)

Two species of petrel breed in
Iceland, the **Leach's petrel**
(Oceanodroma leucorhoa)
and **storm petrel** (Hydro-
bates pelagicus). Their
breeding grounds are very
limited, although there
are considerable num-
bers of both species. The
Leach's petrel breeds
almost exclusively in
the Westman Islands.

Leach's petrel

The two above families,
fulmars/shearwaters
and petrels, belong to
the order of **tubenoses**
(Procellariiformes), whose
name is derived from the nostrils
which have evolved into one or two tubes on the
bird's beak.

All these species except the fulmar spend the winter
at sea.

GANNETS
(Sulidae)

The gannet (Sula bassana) breeds in various places
in the south, east and north of Iceland. The largest
colony, on Eldey island off Reykjanes in the southwest, comprises about 15 thousand breeding pairs.
There is also a considerable gannet population in the
Westman Islands. Gannets can often be seen along the
coast in summer, while in the winter they usually
keep to the high seas.

CORMORANTS
(Phalacrocorasidae)

Cormorants are related to gannets, as indicated by the fact that all four toes are webbed. Cormorants, like gannets, belong to the order of pelicans (Pelicaniformes).

The cormorant (Phalacrocorax carbo) nests primarily on skerries and small islands off the west coast, while juveniles may be seen in many coastal areas.

The shag (Phalacrocorax aristotelis), like the cormorant, nests almost exclusively off the west coast, but its nesting habits are somewhat different.

Cormorant

HERONS
(Ardeidae)

The heron (Ardea cinerea) is a regular winter visitor to Iceland; these are normally juveniles, probably from the west of Norway. Herons normally stay close to the coast, but they may occasionally be seen far inland by lakes or rivers that have not frozen.

WATERFOWL
(Anatidae)

This category of Icelandic breeding birds is highly diverse, and it is interesting that such a variety of species should be found in Iceland.

The **whooper swan** (Cygnus cygnus) nests in all parts of the country, especially on heathland, and is very noticeable in summer. In late summer, immature birds gather in groups, which may be numerous, and moult. Such moulting locations are, for instance, at Álftafjörður (Swan Fjord) on the Snæfellsnes peninsula, Álftafjörður in the east, and Neslandavík at Lake Mývatn. Most Icelandic whooper swans are migrants, but small groups of them may often been seen off the southwest coast, and also adjacent to springs in the northeast and the south.

Whooper swan

Two goose species breed in Iceland, the **greylag goose** (Anser anser) and **pink-footed goose** (Anser brachyrhinchus).

The **greylag goose** breeds in lowland areas all over the country, and breeding colonies in marshy areas are often very densely populated.

The **pink-footed goose** breeds mostly at altitudes of over 400m, generally in quite large colonies. The colony at Þjórsárver, an area of tundra under the Hofsjökull glacier, is the largest known colony of pink-footed goose; the birds that breed in Iceland comprise the vast majority of the species.

Pink-footed goose

Both species are migrants that leave Iceland in late October. Greylag geese are known to remain through the winter, normally in the southwest; these birds generally originate from the Lake in Reykjavík.

Three other species, the **whitefronted goose** (Anser albifrons), **barnacle goose** (Branta leucopsis) and **brent goose** (Branta bernicla) pass through Iceland in spring and autumn; in addition, a few pairs of barnacle geese have bred in Iceland in recent decades.

In spring and autumn, the **white-fronted goose** is most often seen in marshy areas of the south and west, and the Mýrar and Borgarfjörður region. White-fronted geese that stop in Iceland are often the targets of hunters, although the same goose populations are protected in other countries.

Barnacle geese stop in spring in the north of Iceland, in Skagafjörður and the east of Húnavatnssýsla, while in autumn they are generally found in Vestur-Skaftafellssýsla in the southeast.

The brent goose differs considerably from the other goose species in behaviour patterns. They tend to gather on beaches and mudflats, especially in the west. The brent goose population is apparently now recovering from a decline that took place around the middle of 20th century. Populations of greylag goose and pink-footed goose are also rising.

Ducks may be classified into several groups according to their characteristics. The first are **dabbling ducks**.

The mallard (Anas platyrhynchos) is by far the commonest. Mallards nest in all parts of the country, in lowland areas, while during the winter they tend to be found in coastal areas, especially in the south and southwest.

Eurasian teal

The distribution pattern of **the Eurasian wigeon** (Anas penelope) is similar to that of the mallard, except that it is commonest in the northeast, while the opposite is true of the mallard. Both species are to some degree migrants, but the Eurasian wigeon, like the mallard, may be seen on the south-coast in winter.

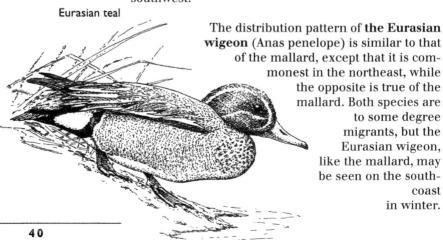

The **Eurasian teal** (Anas crecca) breeds all over the country in favourable environments. Most teals are migrants, but some stay the winter in the south and southwest.

The **gadwall** (Anas strepera) is rare except at and around Lake Mývatn, although a few pairs breed else-where, e.g. in the Reykjavík area. Most gadwalls are migratory.

The **pintail** (Anas acuta), which breeds all over the country, though in small numbers, is exclusively migratory.

The **shoveler** (Anas clypeata) is a recent addition to Iceland's breeding birds. The first shoveler nest was found in Iceland around 1930, and the shoveler is found mainly in the Aðaldalur and Kelduhverfi regions of the north. All shovelers are migrants.

Diving ducks are a diverse group that comprise several genera.

The **Scaup** (Aythya marila) is common in all parts of the country while the **tufted duck** (Aythya fuligula) can be found in most areas except the uplands. The area of Lake Mývatn is the primary breeding area for both species, although a few individuals of both species spend the winter in the southwest. The tufted duck is a fairly recent arrival in Iceland, and did not begin breeding regularly until around 1900.

Tufted duck

The **Pochard** (Aythya ferina) is a close relative of the scaup and tufted duck, and is also the third duck species to have arrived in Iceland this century. A handful of pairs have nested at Lake Mývatn since the 1960s.

The **Barrow's goldeneye** (Bucephala islandica) is unusual in that it is an American species, whose only European breeding ground is in Iceland. The Barrow's goldeneye breeds almost exclusively in the area of Lake Mývatn and the Laxá river, although they may often be seen in winter in spring areas of the northeast and south.

The **goldeneye** (Bucephala clangula), a close relative of the Barrow's goldeneye, is a fairly common winter visitor. They may often be seen on Lake Mývatn in summer, and e.g. by the river Sog and the Skerjafjörður bay (to the south of Reykjavík) in the winter.

Harlequin duck

The **harlequin duck** (Histrionicus histrionicus) is another American species among Iceland's breeding birds. Harlequin are found on fast-flowing rivers both in the breeding season and into the summer. In late June, however, the drakes go out to sea, and by early September most harlequins are out at sea, where they spend the winter. They tend to remain near surf-washed shores, e.g. Reykjanes and Snæfellsnes.

The **common scoter** (Melanitta nigra) is yet another species that is found in the breeding season almost exclusively around Lake Mývatn. Its habitat is ponds and small lakes. In the summer the common scoter is often seen on the sea in the East Fjords, e.g. large groups at Bakkafjörður in the spring. The common scoter is a migrant.

The **long-tailed duck** or **oldsquaw** (Clangula hyemalis) is a typical highland bird, that flies to its breeding grounds as soon as the lakes thaw in spring. Otherwise they generally remain at sea, and they also breed in some places on the coast. During the winter they are usually easy to find in most coastal areas.

The eider (Somateria mollissima) is the only Icelandic duck species that is found almost exclusively at sea. They are rarely seen inland, although they occasionally travel up large rivers. Eider colonies are situated all around the country, and are generally quite dense. There may be thousands of nests in a single colony. Eider colonies seem to thrive best where the birds are protected by man, who claims the down from their nests in return. The relationship is thus mutually beneficial.

The king eider (Somateria spectabilis) is closely related to the eider. This is an Arctic species that is often seen among eiders in the winter, and also in summer, when the king eider drakes mate with female eiders.

Two species of mergansers breed in Iceland; their behaviour patterns are different.

The goosander (Mergus merganser) nests by rivers, and occasionally by lakes where fish is plentiful. Some goosanders remain on rivers and lakes that do not freeze over in winter, generally at the estuary. Many anglers have an aversion to goosanders, which they claim eat salmon and trout smolts. This species has been in decline in Iceland, and it may be in danger of extinction if the trend continues.

Red-breasted merganser

The red-breasted merganser (Mergus serrator) is in a stronger position, and is far more common than the goosander. Red-breasted mergansers are found close to lakes and the sea, and live mostly on stickleback. They are found in all regions of the country, but are quite sparsely distributed. In the winter, red-breasted mergansers are found at the coast.

Finally, two more American species should be mentioned, the **American wigeon** (Anas americana) and **ruddy duck** (Oxyura jamaicensis) which are seen every year at Lake Mývatn; ruddy ducks have also bred there. The shelduck (Tadorna tadorna) is seen as well from time to time, and has been known to breed in Iceland.

EAGLES
(Accipitridae)

The white-tailed eagle (Haliaeetus albicilla) is the only eagle species among Iceland's breeding birds. Eagles used to breed all around the country, but by 1900 the eagle population was in danger of extinction; farmers, who believed the eagle preyed on their livestock, had made strenuous efforts to exterminate them. In 1913, The white-tailed eagle was protected by law; at this point, only a handful of pairs of eagles remained in the west, particularly Breiðafjörður and the West Fjords. The eagle population has risen slightly in recent decades, and it has also enlarged its area of distribution to the south, along the west coast. In spite of this, the eagle population is still far smaller than it was a century ago, and in recent years it has remained almost constant. It is believed to be vital to ensure protection of the species, if the population is not to fall again. Each pair of eagles requires extensive territory to support itself and its offspring, and during the breeding season the white-tailed eagle is highly sensitive to disturbance. The smallest disruption may lead them to abandon their eggs and chicks, and it is prohibited to approach an eagle's eyrie at breeding season. In the autumn and winter, white-tailed eagles may be seen in most areas, but most keep to their favourite habitat in the west, Breiðafjörður, Mýrar and the West Fjords.

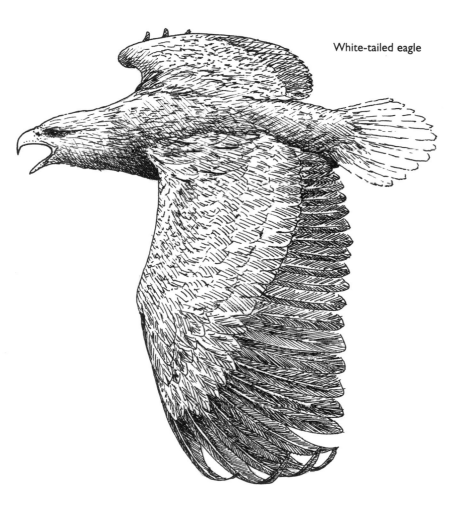

White-tailed eagle

FALCONS
(Falconidae)

The **gyr falcon** (Falco rusticolus) breeds in all regions of the country, but especially in the north. It is highly dependent upon its favourite prey, the ptarmigan, and so is most likely to be found where ptarmigans are present. The gyr falcon is most noticeable in autumn, when the population is at its largest, and juveniles travel widely. The gyr falcon is exclusively a resident species in Iceland. These splendid birds are a favourite with birdwatchers. In olden times, the falcon was a princely possession, and they **Merlin** were trapped, exported, and trained for hunting. The falcon has been a protected species since 1940; however, in spite of severe penalties, there have been attempts at stealing their eggs and chicks.

Greenlandic gyr falcons are occasionally seen in Iceland; these are much lighter in colour, almost white.

The **merlin** (Falco columbarius) is a close relative of the gyr falcon, but with different habits, The merlin is found all over the country, and is less noticeable than the gyr falcon. Most merlins are migratory, though some remain in Iceland during the winter.

GROUSE
(Tetraonidae)

The **ptarmigan** (Lagopus mutus) is Iceland's only wild grouse species, generally found where vegetation is plentiful. Ptarmigans are fairly common breeders among heather, e.g. on the heaths of the north. During the winter, ptarmigans disperse around the country, but generally inland, close to the snow-line, if the lowlands are free of snow. They move about in groups of varying size, living on a variety of vegetation. When snow is heavy, they seek food in birch copses.

RAILS AND COOTS
Rallidae

The water rail (Rallus aquaticus) is the only member of the Rallidae that once bred regularly in Iceland. The water rail's habitat is in marshes and estuaries, and this species is now at risk. Indeed, it is doubtful whether the water rail can be counted as an Icelandic breeding bird any longer since no water rail nest has been found for many years. Some of these birds, believed to be vagrants from neighbouring countries, can be seen here each winter.

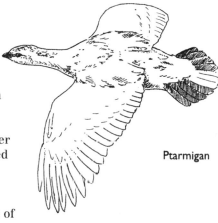

Ptarmigan

The coot (Fulic atra) is of the same family as the water rail. It is a common vagrant, and has bred in Iceland a few times. Coots may be seen in winter mainly on ponds and lakes that have not frozen.

OYSTERCATCHERS
Haematopodidae

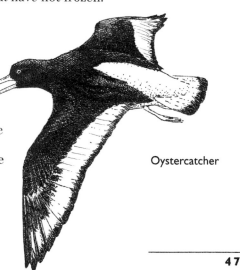

The oystercatcher (Haematopodus ostralegus) is common all around the country's coasts, but it is not exclusively a shore bird. In the south, for instance, it often nests on roadsides far inland. Most oystercatchers are migrants, but in winter flocks of them may be seen in the south and west.

Oystercatcher

WADERS
Charadriidae

The **ringed plover** (Charadrius hiaticula) is primarily a shore bird, like the oystercatcher. It nests exclusively in sand and gravel, normally near the sea but also inland in favourable conditions, e.g. on gravel banks. The ringed plover arrives in Iceland in late April, and departs for southern climes by the end of October.

Golden plover

The **golden plover** (Pluvialis apricaria) is one of Iceland's favourite migrants. They are common all over the country in lowland areas, especially among heather and in dry land with plenty of vegetation. The first golden plovers arrive at the end of March, when they are warmly welcomed by Icelanders, as they are regarded as harbingers of spring. Many remain until November, or even longer. In late summer golden plovers gather together on farmland to wait for favourable conditions for their migration.

The **lapwing** (Vanellus vanellus) is not among Iceland's true breeding birds, although lapwing nests have been found quite often.

Dunlin

SNIPE FAMILY
Scolopacidae

The **dunlin** (Calidris alpina), which is believed to be the commonest of Icelandic waders, is found in marshy areas, in mountains and lowlands alike. It is exclusively a migrant. In spring and autumn, many passage migrants of the same species pass through Iceland, and the species then becomes very noticeable on the shore.

The black-tailed godwit (Limosa limosa) was in the past found only in the south, but it has dispersed around the country during the 20th century. It is still commonest in the south, and nests mostly in marshes. The birds arrive in Iceland in May, and leave again in August.

The bar-tailed godwit (Limosa lapponesa), closely related to the black-tailed variety, is seen from time to time on the shore outside the breeding season; numbers are always small.

The whimbrel (Numenius phaeopus) winters in Africa, and migrates to Iceland in May, flying directly to its breeding grounds, The species' ideal habitat is in lowland heaths. The whimbrel departs again by early September.

The curlew (Numenius arquata), a close relative of the whimbrel, is an annual winter visitor. In recent years the curlew has bred in the northwest, but this is probably only a single pair of birds.

The snipe (Gallinago gallinago) is common all around the country in lowland areas. Its habitat is in marshes and moors, but also in copses and birchwoods, where they exist. Most snipes are migrants, but the occasional bird will remain through the winter, especially at the shore or on lakes and rivers that have not frozen.

Close relatives of the snipe, **the jack snipe** (Lymnocryptes minimus) and **woodcock** (Scolopax rusticola) are also seen in Iceland from time to time.

The redshank (Tringa totanus) is very common in the lowlands. It nests largely in grassy fields and moors, and apparently shuns copses and wet marshes. The Redshank is not exclusively a migrant, as several hundred birds spend the winter on the shores of the south.

The **purple sandpiper** (Calidris maritima) breeds in many parts of the country, especially in the highlands, but also in barren areas of the lowlands. This is a robust bird, that passes the winter on the coast.

Phalaropes (Phalaropodinae), the **grey phalarope** (Phalaropus fulicarius) and **red-necked phalarope** (Phalaropus lobatus), are today also regarded as members of the snipe family.

The former species, the grey phalarope, seems to be disappearing as an Icelandic breeding bird; only 40 to 50 breeding pairs remain. The grey phalarope makes only a brief stay of about two months in the summer.

Red-necked phalarope

The red-necked phalarope, on the other hand, is common in marshy areas all over the country, although the population has fallen in recent decades. They nest by ponds and marshy estuaries. The red-necked phalarope gathers food by unusual means, swimming around in circles and stirring up food, which it then picks out of the water. The winter home of this bird has not been firmly identified, but birds of both species that breed in Iceland are believed to winter in the south Atlantic.

The turnstone (Arenaria interpres) is a passage migrant that may be seen on the shore at all times of year, but especially in spring and autumn, and some remain in Iceland all year round. **The knot** (Calidris canutus) and **sanderling** (Calidris alba) stop over in Iceland in spring and autumn, mainly on the west coast. **The wood sandpiper** (Tringa glareola) has been known to breed in Iceland, but is very rarely seen.

SKUAS
Stercorariidae

The great skua (Stercorarius skua) is commonest on the sandy plains south of the Vatnajökull glacier. One of the largest great skua colonies in the northern hemisphere is situated on Breiðamerkursandur in the southeast; the distribution area of the great skua in the south has grown, and it now stretches as far west as Þorlákshöfn in the south-west. Smaller colonies exist in other regions, e.g. by Héraðsflói and in Öxarfjörður in the east and north. The great skua gathers food both at sea and on land. They often seize food from other birds, and also hunt other birds for food. They are famed for their ferocious protection of their eggs and chicks. In summer The great skua is often seen along the coast. In winter they remain on the high seas, returning to the coast in early spring.

Great skua

The arctic skua or **parasitic jaeger** (Stercorarius parasiticus) is a common breeding bird all over the country. They nest in low-lying areas, marshes and sandy areas; their food-gathering methods are similar to those of the great skua. They arrive at their breeding ground in the second half of May, leaving in the early autumn.

Two other species, **the pomarine skua** (Stercorarius pomarinus) and **long-tailed skua** (Stercorarius longi-caudus), are occasionally seen in Iceland in the summer, on their migration to their breeding grounds farther north.

GULLS
Laridae

Seven species of Icelandic breeding birds belong to the gull family, four of which have arrived during the 20th century.

The great black-backed gull (Larus marinus) was until recently the most numerous of Icelandic gulls, but its population has dropped considerably in recent years. It nests mostly by the sea. The great black-backed gull is a resident, generally seen on the south and west coasts.

The glaucous gull (Larus hyperboreus) is found almost exclusively on the west coast, where it nests in colonies, large or small, on steep slopes. Glaucous gull colonies can be discerned at some distance; vegetation there is a vivid green, thanks to the guano provided by the birds.

Common gull

The lesser black-backed gull (Larus fuscus) began to breed in Iceland in the 1930s, and has spread fast, especially in the south and west. The lesser black-backed gull is a migrant that arrives in Iceland in late February or early March, one of the first arrivals in spring.

The herring gull (Larus argentatus) arrived in Iceland at about the same time as the lesser black-backed gull. They are commonest in the East Fjords, but have gradually spread through the south and north. Most are residents.

The common gull (Larus canus) is also a new addition to the breeding birds of Iceland, first arriving in the 1930s. The first common gull nest was found in 1960, near Reykjavík. Common gulls are most numerous in the Eyjafjörður region of the north.

The **black-headed gull** (Larus ridibundus) began breeding in Iceland in the early 20th century, and is now a common breeding bird all over the country, both at the coast and inland. They are most numerous in the southwest and the north. The black-headed gull generally nests in dense colonies along with other birds, mainly the arctic tern. Black-headed gulls are generally migratory, but many remain through the winter.

The **kittiwake** (Rissa tridactyla) is very common all around the country. It differs from most gulls in that it nests either on perpendicular cliff faces or low cliffs, along with auks and fulmars. Kittiwakes wander the north Atlantic in winter, and sometimes farther south, as far as Africa.

The **Iceland gull** (Larus glaucoides) is a common winter visitor, especially on the north and west coast. **The ivory gull** (Pagophila eburnea) is also seen occasionally in winter.

TERNS
Sternidae

The **arctic tern** (Sterna paradisaea) is a close relative of the gull. It spends the winter on the shores of the south Atlantic and the Antarctic, and comes to Iceland in early May. Arctic terns breed all over the country, even in the highlands. The largest arctic tern colonies are on the coast; nests may number thousands in a single colony. In late August, they set off again across the Atlantic to their winter home, flying a total of about 40 thousand kilometres every year.

Arctic tern

Another species of tern, the **black tern** (Chlidonias niger), is an occasional visitor. It has occasionally bred in Iceland, but is otherwise a very rare vagrant.

AUKS
Alcidae

Six species of auks breed on the shores of Iceland. These are the ultimate sea birds; they only come ashore to nest and care for their young until they are old enough to look after themselves, or to return to the sea with their parents.

Guillemot

The guillemot or **murre** (Uria aalge), **Brünnich's guillemot** or **thick-billed murre** (Uria lomvia) and razorbill (Alca torda) are all closely related and have a similar lifestyle. In the spring these species gather in their hundreds of thousands on birdcliffs to breed. In late July and early August, the birds then return to the sea with their young. They stay at sea all winter, but often close to the coast.

The puffin (Fratercula arctica) is by far the commonest of Iceland's auk species. Breeding pairs of puffins number in the millions, and the major breeding location for puffins is in the Westman Islands. Puffins lay their eggs in burrows which they dig in the turf of islands and cliffs, and also in cracks and fissures in screes and birdcliffs. The birds leave their burrows in early August, and have usually departed for the ocean by September.

The black Guillemot (Ceppus grylle) nests among rocks. In the winter the black guillemot is found closer to the coast than other auks, and is often seen just off the shore.

The little auk (Alle alle) is one of the rarest of Iceland's breeding birds; Iceland is at the southernmost limit of its distribution area. The remaining breeding pairs on Grímsey island, off Iceland's north coast, can be counted on the fingers of one hand. The little auk is, however, a common breeding bird in the Arctic Ocean, and is often swept to Iceland's shores in northerly winds.

Most species of auks, with the exception of the little auk, are found all around the country at all seasons. The Brünnich's guillemot and the puffin are rarely seen close to the shore in winter.

PIGEONS AND DOVES
Columbidae

No wild species of pigeon or dove is a regular breeder in Iceland. **The wood pigeon** (Columba palumbus) has, however, bred in Iceland a few times. Other species that have been seen from time to time are **The turtle dove** (Streptopelia turtur) and **collared turtle dove** (Streptopelia decaocto). The latter species has also been known to breed in Iceland.

OWLS
Strigidae

The snowy owl (Nyctea scandiaca) was in the past a regular breeder in Iceland, but the bird's status as an Icelandic breeding bird is now in some doubt, as no nest has been found for some years. In Iceland the snowy owl lives mostly on ptarmigan, goslings and other birds. The snowy owl, though rarely seen, is a regular annual visitor, especially in the north. These are almost certainly all sterile birds from Greenland.

The short-eared owl (Asio flammeus) is a fairly recent addition to Iceland's breeding bird species; the first nest was found in the south early in the 20th century. In Iceland the short-eared owl lives mostly on

Raven

fieldmice and small birds. The short-eared owl is seen most frequently in shrubland in the north. They also seem to be at home in marshland with abundant vegetation, e.g. around Lake Mývatn. Most short-eared owls are migrants, although some remain during the winter. Some short-eared owls from abroad also visit Iceland in winter, along with a close relative, **the long-eared owl** (Asio otus).

CROWS
Corvidae

The raven (Corvus corax) is the largest of Iceland's passerines. The Raven breeds all over the northern hemisphere, and is common all over the country except in the highlands. In Iceland the raven normally nests on cliffs, but occasionally on the outside of buildings and other man-made structures. Ravens are highly adaptable with regard to feeding. In the summer they prey on the chicks and eggs of other bird species, while in winter they live mostly on carrion and other waste. Ravens prey on eider colonies and birdcliffs, so they tend to be unpopular, and various measures have been taken to exterminate them. On the other hand, the raven has featured in Icelandic folklore since time immemorial, as a symbol of wisdom and portent. Ravens are resident in Iceland.

Two related species, **the rook** (Corvus frugilegus) and **jackdaw** (Corvus monedula), are annual vagrants that often come to Iceland in groups in the autumn.

THRUSHES
Turdidae

The redwing (Turdus iliacus) is common all over the country in the summer. In late autumn Redwings leave the country, but a growing number remain through the winter, no doubt due to growing afforestation and horticulture in recent decades.

Redwing

The wheatear (Oenanthe oenanthe), ᴗ relative of the redwing, arrives in Iceland in May and is common all over the country. Wheatears nest mostly in rocky areas and screes. They are exclusively migratory, their winter home being in Africa.

The blackbird (Turdus merula) and **fieldfare** (Turdus pilaris) are frequent winter visitors, that have bred quite often in Iceland.

WAGTAILS
Motacillidae

White wagtail

The white wagtail (Motacilla alba) breeds all over the country close to human habitation, and also by rivers and brooks on the coast. It is exclusively a migrant, with its winter home in West Africa.

The meadow pipit (Anthus pratensis) is the commonest of Icelandic passerines, which breeds all over the country, mostly in moorland. Meadow Pipits are migrants, that spend the winter in southwestern Europe.

The rock pipit (Anthus petrosus) is a new arrival in Iceland, which has bred in the country for the past few years, but it is very rarely spotted.

WRENS
Troglodytidae

The wren (Troglodytes troglodytes), a resident species, is the smallest of Icelandic birds. Their habitat is in birchwoods and copses. Wrens normally spend the winter close to streams that have not frozen over, and on the shore. The Icelandic Wren is a separate subspecies, a little larger and darker in colour than wrens in neighbouring countries.

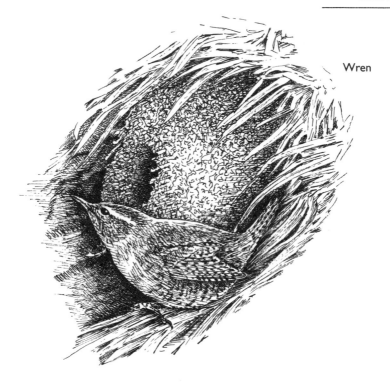

Wren

STARLINGS
Sturnidae

The starling (Sturnus vulgaris) began to breed in Iceland around 1940, first in the southeast, but from 1960 in the southwest also. From here, the Starling has dispersed throughout the south and west. They are generally found close to human habitation, and are now commonest in the Reykjavík area. Starlings are a resident species.

SPARROWS
Passeridae

The house sparrow (Passer domesticus) is one of Iceland's rarest breeding birds, although very common in neighbouring countries. House sparrows were first known to breed in Reykjavík around 1960, and a handful of pairs now breed in Öræfasveit in the southeast.

FINCHES
Fringillidae

The redpoll (Carduelis flammea) makes its home in birchwoods in the north and east. With increasing arboriculture, the redpoll has settled in urban areas, e.g. in the capital area. The redpoll is a resident species.

Redpoll

BUNTINGS
Emberizidae

The snow bunting (Plectrophenax nivalis) is commonly found in the highlands, but also breeds elsewhere, such as in lava fields and on rugged territory. Most Icelandic snow buntings are resident, but they sometimes travel abroad.

The brambling (Fringilla montefringilla), **swallow** (Hirundo rustica) and **house martin** (Delichon urbica) are common vagrants, that have occasionally bred in Iceland.

Brambling

Only about 10 species of passerines breed regularly in Iceland, and another handful from time to time. Iceland differs in this respect from the neighbouring countries, where passerines are the commonest breeding birds. Various passerines that are common in the neighbouring countries appear as vagrants in Iceland from time to time: **The waxwing** (Bombycilla garullus), **robin** (Erithacus rubecula), **song thrush** (Turdus philomelos), **garden warbler** (Sylvia borin), **blackcap** (Sylvia atricapilla), **chiffchaff** (Phylloscopus collybita), **willow warbler** (Phylloscopus trochilus), **goldcrest** (Regulus regulus), **chaffinch** (Fringilla coelebs) and **crossbill** (Loxia curvirostra).

These birds are mostly seen in autumn.

LIST OF ICELANDIC BIRDS
and where to find them

Around 330 species of birds have been seen in Iceland, of which 122 are included in this list. The species listed below are regular breeding birds of Iceland unless otherwise noted. Several other species occurring in the country are included also, identified as follows: (V) Vagrant, (PM) Passage Migrant, (HB) has bred in Iceland at least once but does not breed there regularly, (WV) Winter Visitor.

The numbers that appear after the name of a species in the list indicate in which areas the birds may be seen, with reference to the bird-watching areas described in this book. An area number in bold type indicates that the species is easily found in the relevant area. An area number in thin type indicates that there is some likelihood of seeing the species in the area, although it is far from certain. If one or more numbers do not appear after the species, it may be assumed that the species is, for whatever reason, unlikely to be observed in the relevant area(s).

It should be reiterated that when a specific area is indicated, this is normally with reference to the period April-September. It is often difficult to assess to probability of seeing a particular bird species, or where it is most likely to be found. Hence for many bird species, one or more area numbers do not appear on the list.

species	area	species	area
Divers:		*Petrels:*	
1. Great northern diver/		8. Leach's petrel	10
Common loon	1,**3**,**5**,**6**,7,11,**12**	9. Storm petrel	10
2. Red-throated diver/			
Red-throated loon	1,2,3,**4**,**5**,**6**,**7**,**8**,11,**12**	*Gannets:*	
		10. Gannet	**1**,3,4,**7**,**9**,**10**,11
Grebes:			
3. Slavonian horned/grebe	**2**,**3**,**6**,**7**,8	*Cormorants:*	
		11. Cormorant	**1**,**2**,**3**,**4**,**5**,7,9,10,**11**
		12. Shag	**1**,**2**,**3**,**4**,5,7,9,10,**11**
Fulmars and shearwaters:			
4. Fulmar	**1**,**2**,**3**,**4**,**5**,**7**,**8**,9,10,**11**	*Herons:*	
5. Manx shearwater	10	13. Heron (WV)	
6. Great shearwater (PM)			
7. Sooty shearwater (PM)		*Waterfowl:*	
		14. Whooper swan	**1**,**2**,**3**,**5**,**6**,**7**,**8**,9,**11**,**12**
		15. Greylag goose	**2**,3,**4**,**5**,**6**,**7**,**8**,9,**11**,**12**
		16. Pink-footed goose	6,7

species	area
17. White-fronted goose (PM)	3
18. Barnacle goose (PM,HB)	8
19. Brent goose (PM)	1,2,3
20. Canada goose (V)	
21. Mallard	**1,2,3**,4,**5,6,7,8,9**,10,**11,12**
22. Eurasian wigeon	1,2,**3**,6,**7,8**,11,12
23. Eurasian teal	**3**,5,**6**,7,8,11,12
24. Pintail	**6**,7
25. Gadwall	2,**6**,7
26. Shoveler	6
27. American wigeon (V)	
28. Scaup	**2,3**,6,**8**
29. Tufted duck	**2,3,6**,8
30. Pochard	
31. Barrow's goldeneye	**6**,12
32. Goldeneye (WV)	
33. Harlequin duck	1,3,**5,6,7**,8,**12**
34. Common scoter	6,7
35. Long-tailed duck/ oldsquaw	**1,2,3**,4,**5,6,7**,11,12
36. Eider	**1,2,3**,4,**5**,7,**8,9,10,11**
37. King eider (V)	
38. Goosander	5,6,12
39. Red-breasted merganser	**1,2,3**,4,**5,6,7**,8,10,**11,12**

Eagles:
42. White-tailed eagle	5

Falcons:
43. Gyr falcon	5,6
44. Merlin	5,6,7,8,12

Grouse:
45. Ptarmigan	3,4,5,6,7,8,12

Rails and coots:
46. Water rail	
40. Ruddy duck (V, HB)	
41. Shelduck (V, HB)	
47. Coot (V, HB)	

species	area
Oystercatchers:	
48. Oystercatcher	**1,2,3,4,5**,7,**8,9**,10,**11**,12
Waders:	
49. Ringed plover	**1,2,3,4,5,7,8,9**,11
50. Golden plover	**1,2,3,4,5,6,7,8,9,10,11,12**
51. Lapwing (V, HB)	
Snipe family:	
52. Dunlin	**1,2,3,4,5,6,7,8,9**,11,**12**
53. Purple sandpiper	**1,2,3,4,5**,7,**8,9**,10,11
54. Knot (PM)	3
55. Sanderling (PM)	1,3
56. Snipe	**1,2,3,4,5,6,7,8,9,10,11,12**
57. Jack snipe (V)	
58. Woodcock (V)	
59. Black-tailed godwit	2,**3**,6,8,9,**11**,12
60. Bar-tailed godwit (PM)	
61. Whimbrel	**1,2,3**,4,**5,6,7,8,9**,10,**11,12**
62. Curlew (WV, HB)	
63. Redshank	**1,2,3,4,5,6,7,8,9,10,11,12**
64. Wood sandpiper (V, HB)	
65. Turnstone (PM)	**1,2,3**,4,5,7,8,9,10,**11**
66. Red-necked phalarope	1,2,**3,4,5,6,7**,8,9,**11,12**
67. Grey phalarope	

Skuas:
68. Great skua	1,**7,8,9,10**,11
69. Arctic skua/parasitic jaeger	1,2,**3,4,5,6,7,8,9,10,11**,12
70. Pomarine skua (PM)	
71. Long-tailed skua (PM)	

Gulls:
72. Great black-backed gull	**1,2,3,4,5**,6,7,**8,9,10,11**,12
73. Glaucous gull	**1,2,3,4,5**,9,**10,11**
74. Lesser black-backed gull	**1,2,3**,4,10,**11**,12

species	area	species	area
75. Herring gull	1,2,**7**,**8**,**9**,10,11	*Waxwings:*	
76. Common gull		100. Waxwing (V)	
77. Black-headed gull	**1**,**2**,**3**,**4**,**5**,**6**,**7**,**8**,**9**,10,11,12	*Wrens:*	
78. Iceland gull (WV)		101. Wren	5,6,7,8
79. Ivory gull (V)			
80. Kittiwake	1,2,**3**,**4**,**5**,7,**8**,**9**,10,11	*Thrushes:*	
Terns:		102. Redwing	**1**,**2**,**3**,4,**5**,**6**,**7**,**8**,**9**,10,**11**,**12**
81. Arctic tern	**1**,**2**,**3**,**4**,**5**,**6**,**7**,**8**,**9**,10,11,12	103. Blackbird (V, HB)	
82. Black tern (V, HB)		104. Fieldfare (V, HB)	
		105. Song thrush (V)	
Auks:		106. Wheatear	1,2,3,4,5,6,7,8,9,11,12
83. Guillemot/murre	**1**,3,4,5,**9**,**10**	107. Robin (V)	
84. Brünnich's guillemot/ Thick-billed murre	**1**,3,4,5,**9**,**10**	*Warblers:*	
85. Razorbill	**1**,3,4,5,10	108. Garden warbler (V)	
86. Puffin	1,2,**3**,**4**,**5**,7,**9**,**10**	109. Blackcap (V)	
87. Black guillemot	1,2,**3**,**4**,**5**,7,10	110. Chiffchaff (V)	
88. Little auk		111. Willow warbler (V)	
		112. Goldcrest (V)	
Pigeons and Doves:			
89. Wood pigeon (V, HB)		*Crows:*	
90. Turtle dove (V)		113. Raven	**1**,**2**,**3**,**4**,**5**,**6**,**7**,**8**,**9**,10,**11**,**12**
91. Collared turtle dove (V, HB)		114. Jackdaw (V)	
		115. Rook (V)	
Owls:			
92. Snowy owl		*Starlings:*	
93. Short-eared owl	6	116. Starling	**1**,**2**,11
94. Long-eared owl (V)			
		Sparrows:	
Swallows		117. House sparrow	
95. Swallow (V, HB)			
96. House martin (V, HB)		*Finches:*	
		118. Redpoll	**2**,**6**,**7**,**8**
Wagtails:		119. Brambling (V, HB)	
97. White wagtail	**1**,**2**,**3**,**4**,**5**,**6**,**7**,**8**,**9**,11,12	120. Chaffinch (V, HB)	
98. Meadow pipit	**1**,**2**,**3**,**4**,**5**,**6**,**7**,**8**,**9**,10,**11**,**12**	121. Crossbill (V)	
99. Rock pipit (V, HB)			
		Buntings:	
		122. Snow bunting	**1**,**2**,**3**,**4**,**5**,6,7